What Can We Do About DEFORESTATION?

David J. Jakubiak

PowerKiDS
press

New York

For Brian Hafkey, a true sportsman who has taught me the awe that lies in a grove of oak trees

Published in 2012 by The Rosen Publishing Group, Inc.
29 East 21st Street, New York, NY 10010

First Edition

Editor: Amelie von Zumbusch
Book Design: Kate Laczynski
Layout Design: Julio Gil

Photo Credits: Cover, pp. 4, 6, 8, 14, 16, 20 Shutterstock.com; p. 10 John Howard/Lifesize/Thinkstock; p. 12 Daniel J. Cox/Stone/Getty Images; p. 18 Harald Sund/Getty Images.

Library of Congress Cataloging-in-Publication Data

Jakubiak, David J.
 What can we do about deforestation? / by David J. Jakubiak. — 1st ed.
    p. cm. — (Protecting our planet)
 Includes index.
 ISBN 978-1-4488-4986-4 (library binding) — ISBN 978-1-4488-5119-5 (pbk.) —
 ISBN 978-1-4488-5120-1 (6-pack)
 1. Deforestation—Juvenile literature. I. Title.
 SD418.J35 2012
 634.9'5—dc22
                          2011000160

Manufactured in the United States of America

CPSIA Compliance Information: Batch #WS11PK: For Further Information contact Rosen Publishing, New York, New York at 1-800-237-9932

CONTENTS

Visiting a forest is a way to learn about the biodiversity of forests firsthand. If there are no forests near you, watch movies or read books about forests.

A Walk Through the Woods

Walk through the woods. Look up to see how tall the trees are. Look down to find the tiniest plants. Smell the air. Listen for animals.

Forests are more than just trees. In the United States, tiny tree frogs and huge wolves can both be found in forests. African forests are home to chimpanzees, gorillas, and forest elephants. In Brazilian forests, monkeys howl, pythons crawl, and sloths sleep. All the living things within a place make up its **biodiversity**. Forests have some of the richest biodiversity on Earth.

Today, forests are being cut down all around the world. The loss of forests is called deforestation. When a forest is cut down, its biodiversity is lost, too.

This deer is in a temperate forest. Earth's forests are home to several kinds of deer. Many live in temperate forests. Others live in tropical rain forests.

Earth's Forests

There are many different kinds of forests on our planet. How hot it gets in a given place and how many seasons there are set the type of forest that grows there. Different kinds of trees and other plants grow in each type of forest.

Tropical rain forests are hot, wet, and have very rich biodiversity. They are found in Asia, Africa, Central America, and South America. The forests in the United States are mostly temperate forests. They have a mix of pine trees and trees with leaves. Some of the forests in California are Mediterranean forests. Most of the trees there are **evergreens**. They do not lose their leaves in the winter.

All plants take in water, carbon dioxide, and sunlight to make energy and oxygen. This happens mostly in the leaves or other green parts of the plant.

Trees Help Us Breathe

When you breathe, you take in **oxygen** and breathe out **carbon dioxide**. Breathing is not the only thing that makes carbon dioxide. Burning fuels makes a lot of carbon dioxide. Scientists now know that all the carbon dioxide we are releasing is changing Earth's **climate**, or weather patterns.

Unlike animals, trees take in carbon dioxide. In fact, they use light, water, and carbon dioxide to make oxygen and energy.

Forests are very important **carbon sinks**. This means they use more carbon dioxide than they release. In fact, forests slow down climate change a bit by taking in some of the carbon dioxide that people make.

DID YOU KNOW?

Rain forests make some of their own rain. Water lost through the leaves in thick forests falls back down as rain. If the forest is lost, the rain will be lost, too.

Wood from trees is used to make many useful and interesting things. This boy is finishing off a shelf he made out of wood.

Woods to Wood

When the first European settlers came to North America, the tall trees they saw amazed them. By that time, most of Europe's giant trees had been cut down. Today, many of North America's forests have been cut down, too.

One reason people cut down forests is to use the wood from the trees. In logging, trees are cut down and turned into **lumber**. Lumber is used to make everything from houses and hardwood floors to chairs and TV stands. Trees are also used to make paper.

Some forests that are cut down for lumber and paper are replanted. Other forests are lost forever.

DID YOU KNOW?

Sometimes, whole forests are cut down in a very short period of time. This is called clear-cutting. People who work with forests argue about whether clear-cutting is a good idea.

This forest in Madagascar is being cleared by the slash-and-burn method.
This is one of the main causes of deforestation in Madagascar.

Slash-and-Burn Agriculture

While forests are sometimes cut down for their trees, they are also cut down to clear land. The cleared land is often turned into farms. Cities and towns are also built on land where forests once grew.

In some parts of the world, farmers clear land by cutting down trees and setting forests on fire. This is called slash-and-burn agriculture. Farmers do this to clear land for cows and other animals. After cows have moved onto cleared land, they make it impossible for the forests to return.

Slash-and-burn agriculture has been going on for centuries. Scientists think that Native Americans using slash-and-burn agriculture may have formed some of North America's grasslands.

You can see the bare earth that was left behind when this part of a forest was cut down. Bare earth like this often washes away in heavy rains.

From Forest to Dirt Patch

When a forest is lost, more than trees disappear. The forest's rich biodiversity is often replaced by fewer kinds of plants and animals.

Forests help stop **erosion**, too. Soil is more easily washed or blown away after a forest has been cut down. This happens because the soil is no longer held in place by tree roots.

In rain forests, the plants and trees hold most of the **nutrients**. Nutrients are things living things need to grow. When a forest is burned and cows move in, these nutrients are quickly lost. After a few years, the land turns hard and dry.

Golden lion tamarins live in Brazil's rain forests. The monkeys are in danger of dying out because the forests they live in are being cut down.

Animals and People in Trouble

The tropical rain forests of Indonesia and Malaysia are home to the orangutan. These forests are being lost to oil palm **plantations**. These are large pieces of land where oil palms are planted. These trees are used to make palm oil. Palm oil is then used to make many fatty snacks. A United Nations study done in 2007 says that wild orangutans will be almost gone by 2040.

Orangutans are not the only animals in trouble. Deforestation is hurting giant pandas in China, gorillas in Africa, and wood turtles in the United States. Animals that live in the forest are in trouble all across the planet.

DID YOU KNOW?

People can be hurt by deforestation, too. Some peoples have lived in certain forests for thousands of years. When these forests are cut down, these people lose their way of life.

These people are visiting the Hoh Rain Forest. This forest has been conserved. It is part of Olympic National Park, in Washington.

How Forests Are Saved

Lots of people understand the importance of forests. Today, people are working to save forests. In many countries, large pieces of forest have been set aside for **conservation**. Keeping these places safe from logging can be hard work. Conserved forests from Madagascar to North Korea to Brazil have suffered deforestation.

People also disagree about how to care for conserved forests. Some countries, including the United States, allow some logging in protected forests.

While some places are trying to save their forests, other places are planting new forests. In Papua New Guinea, a **mangrove forest** is being planted to protect the beach from erosion. These forests grow in watery places.

Where Trees Tower Again

Today, people visit New England's forests each fall to see leaves turn bright colors. There were few forests in New England 150 years ago. They had been cut down to make room for farms.

As factories were built in the 1800s, people moved away from many farms. This let the forests grow back. Animals have returned as well. Moose, black bears, and beavers were almost never seen in Massachusetts 100 years ago. Today, they are fairly common in some parts of the state.

The return of forests and wildlife in New England proves that forests can recover. It takes a long time, though. It also takes people finding ways to live with forests.

All Trees Are Local

There are many ways that you can make the world safe for forests. Learning all you can about forests is a good first step. If you can, visit a forest to learn more about the plants and animals that live there.

There are other ways you can help, too. Try not to waste paper. Always recycle paper, too. When you buy things made of wood, ask where the wood came from. Read food labels. Ask yourself if forests may have been hurt to bring you this food.

Forests are great places to take walks with your family. They are also very important to our planet. The healthier our forests are, the healthier we will all be.

GLOSSARY

biodiversity (by-oh-dih-VER-sih-tee) The number of different types of living things that are found in a certain place on Earth.

carbon dioxide (KAHR-bun dy-OK-syd) An odorless, colorless gas. People breathe out carbon dioxide.

carbon sinks (KAHR-bun SINKS) Things that take in more carbon dioxide than they make.

climate (KLY-mut) The kind of weather a certain place has.

conservation (kon-sur-VAY-shun) Keeping something safe.

erosion (ih-ROH-zhun) The wearing away of land over time.

evergreens (EH-ver-greenz) Shrubs or trees that have green leaves or needles all year long.

lumber (LUM-ber) Wood cut from logs.

mangrove forest (MAN-grohv FAWR-est) A forest of trees that grows in swamps and along rivers.

nutrients (NOO-tree-ents) Food that a living thing needs to live and grow.

oxygen (OK-sih-jen) A gas that has no color or taste and is necessary for people and animals to breathe.

plantations (plan-TAY-shunz) Very large farms where crops are grown.

INDEX

WEB SITES

Due to the changing nature of Internet links, PowerKids Press has developed an online list of Web sites related to the subject of this book. This site is updated regularly. Please use this link to access the list:
www.powerkidslinks.com/pop/deforest/